MW01570910

This notebook belongs to

CPSIA information can be obtained
at www.ICGtesting.com
Printed in the USA
LVHW080503240819
628843LV00012B/412/P